MOVE ABROAD

GOAL SETTING CHECKLIST

PLANNER

Get motivated, get organized and prepared for your international move!

First, GET CLEAR ON YOUR GOALS

1. Where do I want to move?

2. Why is this move important to me?

3. What's getting in the way of my goal?

4. What's my timeline for this move?

5. How will I feel after this move?

Take time to think about why you want to make this move. Get clear on your "why" and write it out. This makes it easier to stay on track with our goals.

where do I want to move?

why is this move important to me?

what's getting in the way of my goal?

what's my timeline for this move?

how will I feel when I make this move?

Action Steps to Take

1

WHERE DO YOU WANT TO MOVE?

- Do you plan to live in a city or the country?

- Research your destination ideas online, in books and articles

- Estimate the costs of living; housing, utilities, transport etc

- Research round trip and one way airfares to your new country

- Research costs to ship household goods online

2

WHY IS THIS MOVE IMPORTANT?

- Are you moving to be closer to loved ones or family? Get into the habit of calling and keeping in touch
- If you're moving for a job, start researching the company or industry you'll be joining once you move
- If you're moving for a lifestyle change or to retire, start thinking about how to make new friends, network and become part of the community you're moving to

3

WHAT'S GETTING IN THE WAY?

- Once you've identified any issues or doubts you have, how can you get over these roadblocks?
- If you're worried about who you're leaving behind, identify how to keep that relationship strong
- Money worries? Identify how you can start saving more.
- Anxiety or fear of change, failure or loss? Look in my <u>Resources</u> for books to help overcome these fears.

4

YOUR MOVING TIMELINE

- 26 weeks is a reasonable timeline to plan a move abroad but what works best for you?
- Will you need to apply for visas or save more before making the move abroad?
- Money worries? Identify how you can start saving more.
- Use my calendar pages or create a move calendar on Google to chart your moving timeline

5

HOW DO YOU WANT TO FEEL?

- Can you astral project into the future and immerse yourself in what it will feel like once you make this move?
- Spend more time in this feeling; create a vision board in Pinterest, on your computer or a wall display
- During the long days of planning, a vision board keeps your goal of a move abroad alive, so make it feel real and amazing!

YES YOU CAN

MOVING TIMELINE ACTION STEPS

Weeks 1, 2, 3 & 4

Research where you want to move
Research residency & visa requirements

Weeks 5 & 6

Plan a pre-move trip to your destination

Weeks 7 & 8

Research jobs, schools as needed.
Research how to move a pet if needed.

Weeks 9 & 10

Contact real estate agents to buy, rent a home and to sell or rent current home

Weeks 11 & 12

Estimate moving costs and create a budget for moving

Weeks 13 & 14

Research transportation, shipping a car, and flights

Weeks 15 & 16

Take pre-move trip

Weeks 17 & 18

Follow up on residency and visa requirements, jobs, schools and where to live

Weeks 19 & 20

Decide what to take, get a firm move quote.
Start selling or dating what you'll leave.

Weeks 21 & 22

Sell and donate household items.
Start packing.

Weeks 23 & 24

Follow up on travel plans to new home.
Pack and donate. Collect personal documents for travel (see checklist)

Weeks 25 & 26

Say goodbye to friends, family.
Finish packing & collect travel documents and finalize move.

PLANNER

YEAR:

January

February

March

April

May

June

July

August

September

October

November

December

Week 1

PLANNER

SUNDAY

MONDAY

TUESDAY

WEDNESDAY

THURSDAY

FRIDAY

SATURDAY

To do

- ☐
- ☐
- ☐
- ☐
- ☐
- ☐
- ☐
- ☐

Tracker

S	M	T	W	T	F	S

S	M	T	W	T	F	S

S	M	T	W	T	F	S

Notes

PLANNER

WEEK:

SUNDAY	
MONDAY	
TUESDAY	
WEDNESDAY	
THURSDAY	
FRIDAY	
SATURDAY	

To do

Tracker

S M T W T F S

S M T W T F S

S M T W T F S

Notes

Week 3

PLANNER

WEEK:

SUNDAY

MONDAY

TUESDAY

WEDNESDAY

THURSDAY

FRIDAY

SATURDAY

To do

- ▢
- ▢
- ▢
- ▢
- ▢
- ▢
- ▢
- ▢

Tracker

S M T W T F S

S M T W T F S

S M T W T F S

Notes

Week 4

PLANNER

SUNDAY

MONDAY

TUESDAY

WEDNESDAY

THURSDAY

FRIDAY

SATURDAY

To do

Tracker

S M T W T F S

S M T W T F S

S M T W T F S

Notes

Week 5

PLANNER

SUNDAY

MONDAY

TUESDAY

WEDNESDAY

THURSDAY

FRIDAY

SATURDAY

To do

-
-
-
-
-
-
-
-

Tracker

S M T W T F S

S M T W T F S

S M T W T F S

Notes

Week 6

PLANNER

SUNDAY

MONDAY

TUESDAY

WEDNESDAY

THURSDAY

FRIDAY

SATURDAY

To do

- [ ]
- [ ]
- [ ]
- [ ]
- [ ]
- [ ]
- [ ]
- [ ]

Tracker

S M T W T F S

S M T W T F S

S M T W T F S

Notes

Week 7

PLANNER   WEEK:

SUNDAY	
MONDAY	
TUESDAY	
WEDNESDAY	
THURSDAY	
FRIDAY	
SATURDAY	

To do

- ....
- ....
- ....
- ....
- ....
- ....
- ....
- ....

Tracker

S M T W T F S

S M T W T F S

S M T W T F S

Notes

....
....
....
....
....
....
....
....
....
....

Week 8

PLANNER

WEEK:

SUNDAY	
MONDAY	
TUESDAY	
WEDNESDAY	
THURSDAY	
FRIDAY	
SATURDAY	

To do

- _____
- _____
- _____
- _____
- _____
- _____
- _____

Tracker

S M T W T F S

S M T W T F S

S M T W T F S

Notes

_____
_____
_____
_____
_____
_____
_____
_____
_____

PLANNER

WEEK:

SUNDAY

MONDAY

TUESDAY

WEDNESDAY

THURSDAY

FRIDAY

SATURDAY

To do

Tracker

S M T W T F S

S M T W T F S

S M T W T F S

Notes

Week 10

WEEK:

SUNDAY

MONDAY

TUESDAY

WEDNESDAY

THURSDAY

FRIDAY

SATURDAY

To do

-
-
-
-
-
-
-

Tracker

S	M	T	W	T	F	S
S	M	T	W	T	F	S
S	M	T	W	T	F	S

Notes

Week 11

PLANNER   WEEK:

SUNDAY

MONDAY

TUESDAY

WEDNESDAY

THURSDAY

FRIDAY

SATURDAY

To do

- [ ]
- [ ]
- [ ]
- [ ]
- [ ]
- [ ]
- [ ]
- [ ]

Tracker

S	M	T	W	T	F	S
S	M	T	W	T	F	S
S	M	T	W	T	F	S

Notes

Week 12

PLANNER

SUNDAY

MONDAY

TUESDAY

WEDNESDAY

THURSDAY

FRIDAY

SATURDAY

To do

Tracker

S M T W T F S

S M T W T F S

S M T W T F S

Notes

Week 13

WEEK:

SUNDAY

MONDAY

TUESDAY

WEDNESDAY

THURSDAY

FRIDAY

SATURDAY

To do

-
-
-
-
-
-
-

Tracker

S	M	T	W	T	F	S
S	M	T	W	T	F	S
S	M	T	W	T	F	S

Notes

Week 14

SUNDAY

MONDAY

TUESDAY

WEDNESDAY

THURSDAY

FRIDAY

SATURDAY

To do

Tracker

S M T W T F S

S M T W T F S

S M T W T F S

Notes

Week 15

PLANNER

SUNDAY	
MONDAY	
TUESDAY	
WEDNESDAY	
THURSDAY	
FRIDAY	
SATURDAY	

To do

- ☐ ....
- ☐ ....
- ☐ ....
- ☐ ....
- ☐ ....
- ☐ ....
- ☐ ....

Tracker

S M T W T F S

S M T W T F S

S M T W T F S

Notes

Week 16

PLANNER

SUNDAY

MONDAY

TUESDAY

WEDNESDAY

THURSDAY

FRIDAY

SATURDAY

To do

- [ ]
- [ ]
- [ ]
- [ ]
- [ ]
- [ ]
- [ ]
- [ ]

Tracker

S M T W T F S

S M T W T F S

S M T W T F S

Notes

Week 17

PLANNER

SUNDAY

MONDAY

TUESDAY

WEDNESDAY

THURSDAY

FRIDAY

SATURDAY

To do

- _____
- _____
- _____
- _____
- _____
- _____
- _____

Tracker

S	M	T	W	T	F	S
S	M	T	W	T	F	S
S	M	T	W	T	F	S

Notes

Week 18

PLANNER   WEEK:

SUNDAY	
MONDAY	
TUESDAY	
WEDNESDAY	
THURSDAY	
FRIDAY	
SATURDAY	

To do

- [ ] _____
- [ ] _____
- [ ] _____
- [ ] _____
- [ ] _____
- [ ] _____
- [ ] _____
- [ ] _____

Tracker

S M T W T F
S M T W T F
S M T W T F

Notes

_____
_____
_____
_____
_____
_____
_____
_____
_____

Week 19

PLANNER

WEEK:

SUNDAY

MONDAY

TUESDAY

WEDNESDAY

THURSDAY

FRIDAY

SATURDAY

To do

- [ ]
- [ ]
- [ ]
- [ ]
- [ ]
- [ ]
- [ ]
- [ ]

Tracker

S M T W T F S

S M T W T F S

S M T W T F S

Notes

Week 20

PLANNER   WEEK:

SUNDAY	
MONDAY	
TUESDAY	
WEDNESDAY	
THURSDAY	
FRIDAY	
SATURDAY	

To do

- [ ]
- [ ]
- [ ]
- [ ]
- [ ]
- [ ]
- [ ]
- [ ]

Tracker

S M T W T F

S M T W T F

S M T W T F

Notes

Week 21

PLANNER

SUNDAY

MONDAY

TUESDAY

WEDNESDAY

THURSDAY

FRIDAY

SATURDAY

To do

Tracker

S	M	T	W	T	F	S

S	M	T	W	T	F	S

S	M	T	W	T	F	S

Notes

Week 22

PLANNER

SUNDAY

MONDAY

TUESDAY

WEDNESDAY

THURSDAY

FRIDAY

SATURDAY

To do

Tracker

S M T W T F

S M T W T F S

S M T W T F

Notes

Week 23

PLANNER

SUNDAY

MONDAY

TUESDAY

WEDNESDAY

THURSDAY

FRIDAY

SATURDAY

To do

- [ ]
- [ ]
- [ ]
- [ ]
- [ ]
- [ ]
- [ ]

Tracker

S	M	T	W	T	F	S
S	M	T	W	T	F	S
S	M	T	W	T	F	S

Notes

Week 24

PLANNER   WEEK:

SUNDAY	
MONDAY	
TUESDAY	
WEDNESDAY	
THURSDAY	
FRIDAY	
SATURDAY	

To do

-
-
-
-
-
-
-
-

Tracker

S M T W T F

S M T W T F

S M T W T F

Notes

Week 25

PLANNER

WEEK:

SUNDAY

MONDAY

TUESDAY

WEDNESDAY

THURSDAY

FRIDAY

SATURDAY

To do

- ☐ ....
- ☐ ....
- ☐ ....
- ☐ ....
- ☐ ....
- ☐ ....
- ☐ ....
- ☐ ....

Tracker

S	M	T	W	T	F	S
S	M	T	W	T	F	S
S	M	T	W	T	F	S

Notes

Week 26

WEEK:

SUNDAY

MONDAY

TUESDAY

WEDNESDAY

THURSDAY

FRIDAY

SATURDAY

To do

-
-
-
-
-
-
-
-

Tracker

S M T W T F

S M T W T F

S M T W T F

Notes

Notes: MOVING QUOTES

Notes: MOVING QUOTES

Notes: MOVING BUDGET

Notes: REAL ESTATE

Notes: RESIDENCY REQUIREMENTS

Notes: PRE MOVE TRIP

Notes: WHAT TO DONATE

Notes: WHAT TO DONATE

Notes: WHAT TO SELL

Notes: WHAT TO SELL

Notes: WHAT TO GIVE AWAY

PACKING LIST

TO PACK+SHIP   **DATE:**

PACKING LIST

TO PACK+SHIP   DATE:

PACKING LIST

TO PACK+TAKE   **DATE:**

UTILITIES| PROPERTY

Company	Email/Phone	Done

INTERNATIONAL MOVERS

MOVE DATE:

1ST MOVE INTERNATIONAL
- Worldwide Shipping
- Palletized Moves
- Comprehensive Insurance
- Weekly Departures
- Countries served: USA, Canada, Australia, New Zealand, South Africa, Cyprus, Malta, Asia, Middle East

BRITANNIA MOVERS INTERNATIONAL
- Ship globally
- Air freight available
- Comprehensive Insurance
- Countries served: USA, Canada, Australia, New Zealand, South Africa, Asia, Middle East and ROW

CLOCKWORK REMOVALS AND STORAGE
- Free International Move Survey • Storage Available
- Door to Door Service
- Full Packing Service
- Marine Transit Insurance
-

PICKFORDS
- Ship globally
- Storage service option
- Comprehensive Insurance
- Pet Moving Service
- Countries served: USA, Canada, Australia, New Zealand, South Africa, Asia, Europe and Middle East

SEVEN SEAS WORLDWIDE
- Ship globally
- Student moving service available
- Online quotes
- Storage Available
- Countries served: USA, Canada, Australia, New Zealand, South Africa, Asia and Middle East

MOVEHUB
Central website where you can get quotes from various shippers

MOVE DATE:

ALTERNATIVE SHIPPING AND MOVING SERVICES FOR SMALLER LOADS

UPAK WESHIP
- ships by container via ocean freight shippers
- offers smaller crates up to a large standard 40 ft container
- offers door to door service
- will deliver a crate to your home, you pack, then they pick it up and take it to a local warehouse. It's then loaded for shipment to a local port and then to your new international home.
- took 4 months from Denver Colorado USA to Southampton, England
- small crate 6 x 6 x 8' cost approx $2000.

MYBAGGAGE.COM
Don't have a lot to move or need it delivered quickly? This service offers door to door luggage shipping.
- can also be used to ship bikes, sporting goods and boxes
- more expensive than UPak but a good alternative if you don't need to ship a lot of goods.

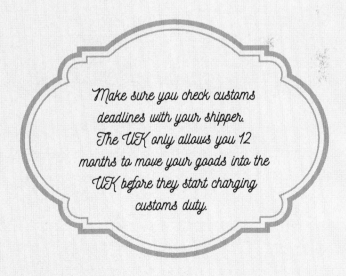

Make sure you check customs deadlines with your shipper. The UK only allows you 12 months to move your goods into the UK before they start charging customs duty.

DOCUMENT CHECKLIST

TO TAKE	FLIGHT INFO:	DATE:

	Passport/Entry Visas
	Birth & Marriage Certificates
	Driving License
	Proof of Citizenship - Residency
	Medical & Dental Records
	Bank & Investment Records | Money Transfer Info
	Home Purchase Records
	Lease Agreements
	Healthcare Plan Details
	Employment Records
	Tax & Accounting Records
	Professional Contacts (Dr, Accountant etc)
	Academic School Records
	Childrens Health Records
	Childrens School Records
	Pet Health Records | Visa Details
	Will or Estate Plan Details

International Flights

DON'T FORGET: STUFF FOR CARRY-ON

- ◯ Travel Documents
- ◯ Prescription medications
- ◯ Sleeping aids
- ◯ Entertainment
- ◯ Vaccination Card

- ◯ Clothes
- ◯ Personal toiletries
- ◯ Electronics
- ◯ Valuables
- ◯ Test Results

BON VOYAGE!

HIPOVERFIFTY.COM

HOW TO MOVE ABROAD IN MIDLIFE WITH STYLE

Made in the USA
Las Vegas, NV
08 February 2022

43487737R00035